Overview *Luka's Campout*

T4-ABM-990

Luka does not get much sleep on his first campout.

Reading Vocabulary Words

noisy
bedtime
tent

High-Frequency Words

shut
sleep
still
eyes
ball
legs
just
lay

Building Future Vocabulary

* These vocabulary words do not appear in this text. They are provided to develop related oral vocabulary that first appears in future texts.

Words:	*tie*	*pitch*	*expression*
Levels:	Gold	Library	Silver

Comprehension Strategy
Making and confirming predictions

Fluency Skill
Using loudness and softness to express emotion

Phonics Skill
Identifying and reading compound words (campout, outside, something, bedtime, himself, goodnight, inside)

Reading-Writing Connection
Copying a phrase

Home Connection
Send home one of the Flying Colors Take-Home books for children to share with their families.

Differentiated Instruction
Before reading the text, query children to discover their level of understanding of the comprehension strategy — Making and confirming predictions. As you work together, provide additional support to children who show a beginning mastery of the strategy.

Focus on ELL
- Show pictures or real items relating to a campout.

- As you hold up an item, sing *I'm going on a campout, and I will bring a _____*. Encourage children to name the item as you pause.

T1

Using This Teaching Version

1. Before Reading

2. During Reading

3. Revisiting the Text

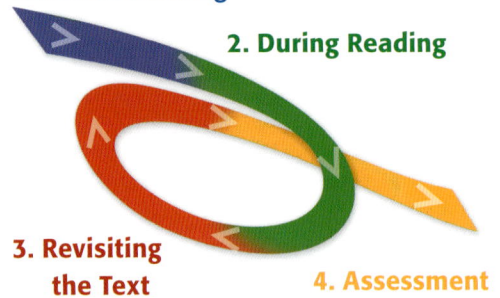

4. Assessment

This Teaching Version will assist you in directing children through the process of reading.

1. **Begin with Before Reading** to familiarize children with the book's content. Select the skills and strategies that meet the needs of your children.

2. **Next, go to During Reading** to help children become familiar with the text, and then to read individually on their own.

3. **Then, go back to Revisiting the Text** and select those specific activities that meet children's needs.

4. **Finally, finish with Assessment** to confirm children are ready to move forward to the next text.

Title I
Chamberlain Elementary
428 N. 5th St.
Goshen, IN 46528

1 Before Reading

Building Background

- Write the word *tent* on the board. Ask children to share what they know about tents and camping. Write responses on chart paper for use later in the text. Correct any misinformation.

- Introduce the book by reading the title, talking about the cover illustration, and sharing the overview.

Building Future Vocabulary

Use Interactive Modeling Card: Meaning Map

- Write the word *pitch* on the Meaning Map. Write a sentence on the board using the word *pitch*. Read the sentence aloud and write it on the Meaning Map.

- Invite children to define the meaning in their own words and record their responses.

Introduction to Reading Vocabulary

- On blank cards write: *noisy*, *bedtime*, and *tent*. Read them aloud. Tell children these words will appear in the text of *Luka's Campout*.

- Use each word in a sentence for understanding.

T2

Introduction to Comprehension Strategy

- Explain that good readers make predictions by connecting information from the text to information they know and experiences they have had.
- Tell children they will be using what they know and new information to make accurate predictions when reading *Luka's Campout.*
- Refer to your list about tents. Ask children to make predictions based on the list, the book cover, and the title page information.

Introduction to Phonics

- Write **campout**, **outside**, **something**, **bedtime**, **himself**, **goodnight**, and **inside** on blank cards.
- Read the words aloud. Ask *What is the name for words that can be separated into two smaller words?* (compound words)
- Choose a word card. Have children identify each word part aloud. Cut the word in half to create two parts. Continue the process with the remaining cards. Have children use the cards to create compound words for additional practice.

Modeling Fluency

- Explain that stories often have punctuation and word clues to tell us how a character feels.
- Say *You are home alone on a dark, stormy night. The power goes out just as you hear a knock at the door. You ask, "Who's there?"* Ask children to tell how they would feel. (scared) Invite children to repeat the last sentence with a tone to match the character's emotions.

2 During Reading

Book Talk
Beginning on page T4, use the During Reading notes on the left-hand side to engage children in a book talk. On page 16, follow with Individual Reading.

During Reading

Book Talk

- Read the title aloud. Ask *Have you ever camped out? What was it like?*

- Have children find the compound word on the cover. *(campout)* Model using the word parts *camp* and *out* to determine the meaning.

- **Comprehension Strategy** Have children look at the title page. Ask *Why do you think the Chapter 2 title is "A Noisy Night"?* (Night has a lot of unfamiliar sounds.)

Turn to page 2 — Book Talk

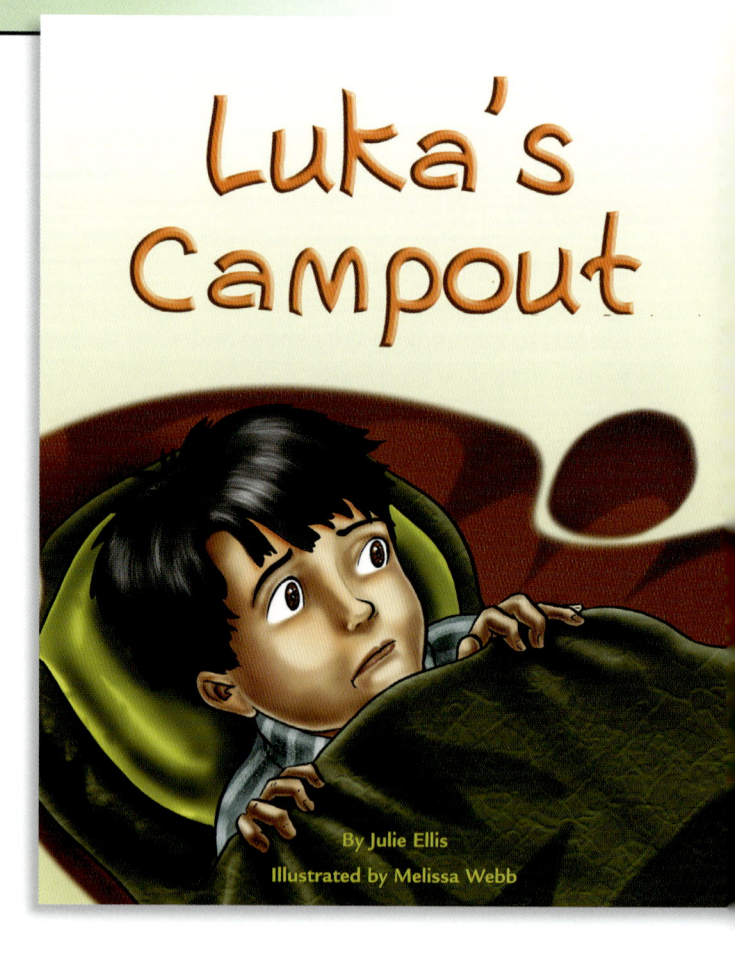

Luka's Campout

By Julie Ellis
Illustrated by Melissa Webb

Luka's Campout

By Julie Ellis

Illustrated by Melissa Webb

Chapter 1	The Tent	2
Chapter 2	A Noisy Night	4
Chapter 3	Jip	14

Revisiting the Text

Future Vocabulary
- Talk about *pitch*ing a tent. Ask *Have you ever set up a tent? How do you do it?* Encourage children to tell the steps in order to *pitch* a tent.
- Have children look at the illustration. Ask *What items do you need to pitch a tent?* (hammer, stakes)

Now revisit pages 2–3

During Reading

Book Talk

- Discuss the story setting. Point to the illustration on page 3 and ask *Where does this story take place?* (outside Grandma's house)

- Have children locate the word *tent* on these pages. Ask *What do you know about the tent from the illustrations?* (It is orange; it has stakes that go into the ground.)

- **Phonics Skill** Point out the words *grandmother, something, tonight,* and *outside.* Prompt children to identify the word parts in each compound word. Guide them to understand the word's meanings by analyzing the smaller parts.

Turn to page 4 – Book Talk

Chapter 1

The Tent

Luka was staying at his grandmother's house.

"I have something for you," said Grandma, and she showed him an orange tent. "This was your dad's when he was a boy."

Revisiting the Text

Grandma helped Luka to put up the tent outside on the grass.

"Can I sleep in the tent tonight, Grandma?" asked Luka. "Please?"

"Yes," said Grandma. "You can have a campout."

"Thanks, Grandma," said Luka. "This will be my first campout. It will be fun!"

3

Future Vocabulary

- Say *How is the word* pitch *used in baseball? Have you ever* pitch*ed a ball? Have you ever hit a home run?*
- Ask *What does* pitch *mean in the sentence* Just pitch *that old shirt.* (Throw it away; put it in the garbage.) *Do you think Luka was glad that Grandma had not* pitch*ed the old tent into the garbage?*

Now revisit pages 4–5

During Reading

Book Talk

- Introduce the term *onomatopoeia.* Talk about words that imitate the sounds associated with them. Say *When I say* hiss, *it sounds like I am hissing. Say* buzz *with me. It sounds like you are buzzing!* Have children identify the words on page 5 that mimic the sound associated with them. (rustle, rustle)

- Invite children to name additional onomatopoeia sounds, such as *pop, quack, meow, splash,* and *crack.*

- **Comprehension Strategy** Say *It is now* bedtime, *and Luka decides to sleep outside in the* tent. *What do you predict is making the rustling* noise *outside Luka's* tent? *How does Luka feel?* (scared) *What picture clues tell you this?* (His eyes are wide; he isn't moving.) *How do you look when you are scared?*

Turn to page 6 — Book Talk

Chapter 2
A Noisy Night

At bedtime, Luka said goodnight to Grandma. Then he went outside to the tent.

Luka went into the tent and got into his sleeping bag.

He shut his eyes, but he did not go to sleep.

4

Revisiting the Text

Rustle, rustle.

Something was outside the tent!
What was it?

Luka stayed very still.
He tried to be brave, but he felt scared.

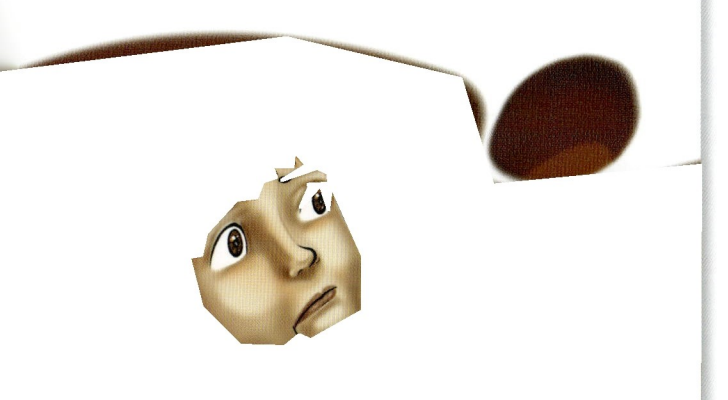

Future Vocabulary
- Discuss facial **expressions**. Call out an emotion and ask children to demonstrate it. Say *Luka's expression tells me he is scared. How do expressions show how you feel?*

Now revisit pages 6–7

5

During Reading

Book Talk

- Say *Look at the illustration on page 7. What was making the rustling noise outside Luka's tent?* (a small animal; an opossum) Some children may incorrectly identify the animal as a rat. If so, explain that an opossum usually moves much more slowly than a rat.

- Explain that some animals are active during the day and others, including opossums, come out at night. Discuss other nocturnal animals such as bats, raccoons, and owls. List them on the board.

- Ask *Would you be scared if you saw an opossum? Why or why not?* Have children tell about a time when they felt very scared at night.

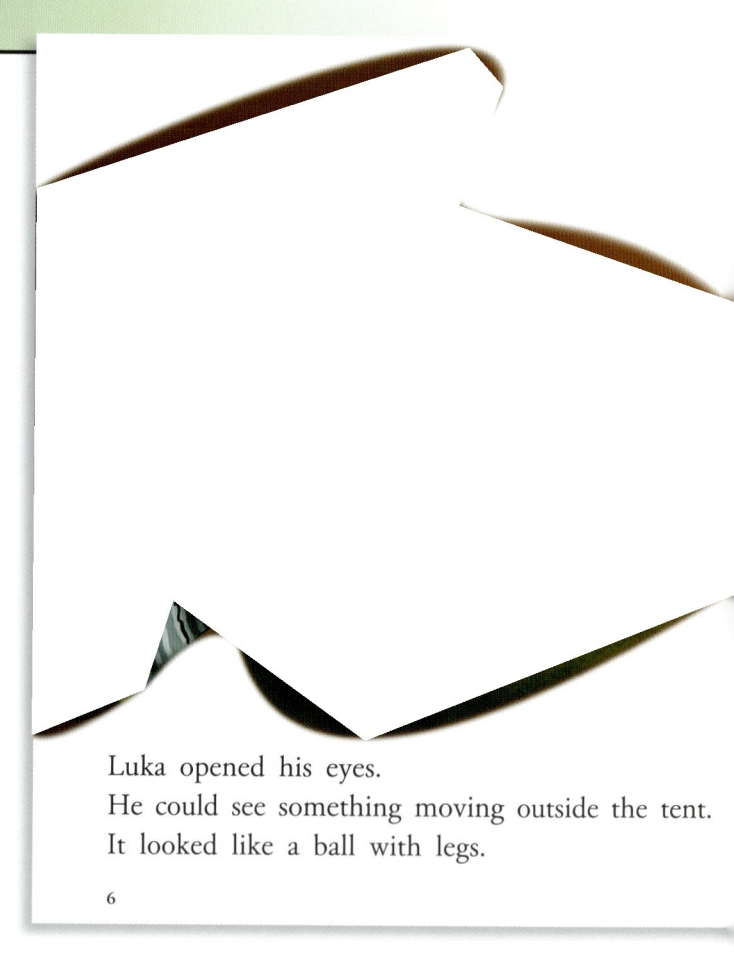

Turn to page 8 — Book Talk

Luka opened his eyes.
He could see something moving outside the tent.
It looked like a ball with legs.

6

Revisiting the Text

Luka smiled to himself.
It was only an opossum!

Luka shut his eyes again,
but he did not go to sleep.

Future Vocabulary
- Say *Show me how Luka's expression changed once he saw it was only an opossum.* Have children mimic the expression and then identify the emotion as relief.

Now revisit pages 8–9

During Reading

Book Talk

- Have children find the onomatopoeia words *crack* and *snap* on these pages.

- **Comprehension Strategy** Say *Look at the shadow on the side of Luka's tent. What do you predict is coming to the tent?*

- Say *Many noises can be heard at night. What kinds of sounds do you think Luka might hear?* (owls, coyotes, frogs, crickets, cars in front of Grandma's house) *How do you think all of these sounds make Luka feel?* (worried, scared)

Turn to page 10 – Book Talk

Crack! Snap!

Luka jumped.
Something was coming,
and it was not an opossum.
It was something big!

What was it?

Revisiting the Text

Future Vocabulary
- Explain how two items may be linked, or tied together. Ask *How is Luka's fear tied to nighttime?* (It is dark, and he can't see what is coming.) *Would he feel like this during the day?* (No, he would be able to see during the day.)

Now revisit pages 10–11

During Reading

Book Talk

- Discuss shadows. Explain that shadows are caused when something blocks the light. Invite children to create shadows using a flashlight and white paper. Then have them describe the shadows and where they occurred.

- Say *Look! It was only Grandma making the shadow on the tent.* Do you think Luka will be able to sleep now that Grandma is with him? Why or why not?

Turn to page 12 – Book Talk

"Hello," said Grandma, looking in the tent. "I just came out to see how you are."

"Grandma," said Luka, "you scared me!"

"Sorry," said Grandma. "Would you like me to sleep out here with you?"

Revisiting the Text

Future Vocabulary

- Talk about *expression* as a way to show your feelings about another person. Ask *How was Grandma's offer to sleep in the tent an expression of her love for Luka?* (It shows she wants to make Luka happy.)

- Ask *How does your family express their love for you? What do they do?* (say "I love you," kiss, hug, do nice things)

Now revisit pages 12–13

"Yes, please," said Luka.

Grandma got into the tent and lay down beside Luka.

Luka shut his eyes, but he did not go to sleep.

During Reading

Book Talk

- **Comprehension Strategy**
  Direct children to look at the illustration and highlighted text on page 12. Ask *Why wasn't Luka able to sleep?* (He saw something scary-looking outside the tent.) *What did he hear? (Thud! Bump!)*

- **Model Fluency** Point out the speech tags *whispered* and *shouted*. Talk about how these words show Luka's emotion. (fear)

- **Comprehension Strategy**
  Point to the illustration on page 13. Ask *What do you think is coming up to the tent now?* Encourage children to predict what will happen next. Discuss the author's use of suspense to hold the reader's interest.

Turn to page 14 – Book Talk

Thud! Bump!

Luka opened his eyes.
Something was coming!

"Grandma," he whispered, but Grandma was asleep.

Luka hid in his sleeping bag.

Luka saw two yellow eyes and a big mouth. Something was coming into the tent!

"**Grandma!**" he shouted.
"Wake up!"

Revisiting the Text

Future Vocabulary

- Say *Luka's tent is* pitch*-black inside. It is hard to see anything. Have you ever been in* pitch*-black darkness? How did it feel?*

- Say *We talked about how* pitch *can mean "to toss," "to throw away," "to put up," and "total," as in* pitch*-blackness. Can you think of other uses for the word* pitch*?* Encourage children to explore other uses of the word *pitch*, such as *to* pitch *a fit,* pitch *a sale,* pitch *headfirst, sing on* pitch*,* and the black tar, also called pitch, used to cover roofs.

Now revisit pages 14–15

During Reading

Book Talk

- Ask *Which word on page 14 tells you what the noisy creature was?* (*Woof* tells you it is a dog.) *How do you think Luka feels when he realizes it was just Grandma's dog, Jip?* (relieved)

- Explain that some animals have eyes that appear to glow at night. Tell children that these animals have a mirror-like layer in their eyes that makes it easier for them to see at night. It reflects the light, which makes the eyes look like they are glowing.

- Say *Now it seems to be noisy inside the tent. Why is it noisy?* (Grandma and Jip are snoring.) *How is snoring shown in the illustration?* (with the letter *z*) *Why do z's represent snoring sounds?* (Snoring can sound like /z/.)

Turn to page 16 – Book Talk

Chapter 3

Jip

"*Woof!*" said the big mouth.

"It's Jip!" said Grandma. "He wants to sleep with us. Jip, lie down!"

14

Revisiting the Text

Grandma shut her eyes and went back to sleep.

Jip shut his eyes and went to sleep, too.

Luka shut his eyes,
but he did not go to sleep for a long time.
He could hear things *inside* the tent.
It was very noisy at night!

Future Vocabulary

- Say *A tie is something a man wears with a suit, but it also has other meanings.* Tie can mean "fasten things together with a rope or string." Tie can also mean "an equal score." *When two people agree to tie the knot, they have decided to get married!*

- Say *On page 15, Grandma and Jip are both snoring. Luka probably thinks their snoring is a tie. Why?* (They're both snoring loudly.)

*Go to page T5 —
Revisiting the Text*

15

During Reading

Book Talk
- Leave this page for children to discover on their own when they read the book individually.

Individual Reading
Have each child read the entire book at his or her own pace while remaining in the group.

Go to page T5 – Revisiting the Text

The next day, Dad came to take Luka home. "Did you like your campout, Luka?" he asked.

"Campout!" said Luka. "It was not a campout. It was a *wake up!*"

16

During independent work time, children can read the online book at:
www.rigbyflyingcolors.com

Revisiting the Text

Future Vocabulary
- Use the notes on the right-hand pages to develop oral vocabulary that goes beyond the text. These vocabulary words first appear in future texts. These words are: *tie*, *pitch*, and *expression*.

Turn back to page 1

Reading Vocabulary Review
Activity Sheet: Word Web

- Have children write the word *noisy* in the center of the Word Web. Then have them look through the text to find words that describe the noises Luka heard.
- Invite children to name items that can make each sound they listed.

Comprehension Strategy Review
Use Interactive Modeling Card: Text Connections Web

- Write *Luka's Campout* in the center box. Review the connections listed at the top. Explain that making connections with the story helps readers understand what they have read.
- With children, complete the boxes using the connection suggestions for guidance.

Phonics Review
- Recall the meaning of compound words as two small words that make up a larger word. Write *rainbow* and *campout* on the board. Have children identify the two smaller words in each.
- Have children look through the text to find compound words. List the words on the board. Ask volunteers to divide the words correctly.

Fluency Review
- Remind children that speech tags and punctuation show readers how to say the words and give clues to the characters' emotions.
- Review the text for word clues. Also note specific speech tags, such as *shouted* and *whispered* on page 12. Have children identify Luka's feelings after each sentence is read.

Reading-Writing Connection
Activity Sheet: Story Map

To assist children with linking reading and writing:
- Have children use the text to fill in the Story Map for *Luka's Campout*.
- Have children use the Activity Sheet to locate an important phrase in the text. Have them copy the phrase and explain why it was important.

T5

4 Assessment

Assessing Future Vocabulary

Work with each child individually. Ask questions that elicit each child's understanding of the Future Vocabulary words. Note each child's responses:

- What does it mean if I have a strong tie to my grandmother?
- How do people show expressions of love?
- Tell me how pitching a tent is different from pitching a baseball.

Assessing Comprehension Strategy

Work with each child individually. Note each child's understanding of making and confirming predictions:

- What did you predict would happen in this story?
- How were your predictions correct? How were they incorrect?
- Do you predict Luka will get more sleep on his next campout? Why?
- Was each child able to predict events and confirm their predictions?

Assessing Phonics

Work with each child individually. Provide children with compound and non-compound words written on cards. Note each child's responses for understanding of compound words:

- Use the following words: *football, paper, candy, carpool, tiptoe, Monday,* and *playpen*
- Did each child identify the compound words and non-compound words?
- Did each child identify the two small words that comprise the compound word?
- Did each child know the meaning of the small words and the compound word?

Assessing Fluency

Have each child read page 12 to you. Note the child's understanding of using loudness or softness to express emotions:

- Did each child read the correct sentence quietly?
- Did each child read the statement with the speech tag *shouted* in a loud voice?
- Did each child read in a normal voice for the sentences not requiring a voice change?

Interactive Modeling Cards

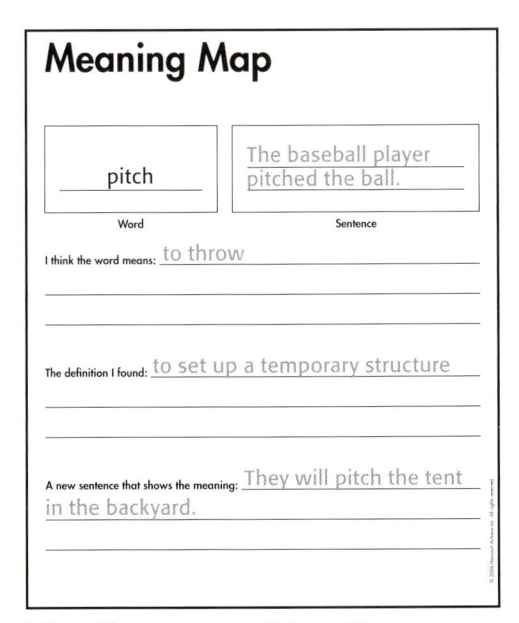

Meaning Map

pitch	The baseball player pitched the ball.
Word	Sentence

I think the word means: to throw

The definition I found: to set up a temporary structure

A new sentence that shows the meaning: They will pitch the tent in the backyard.

Directions: With children, fill in the Meaning Map using the word *pitch*.

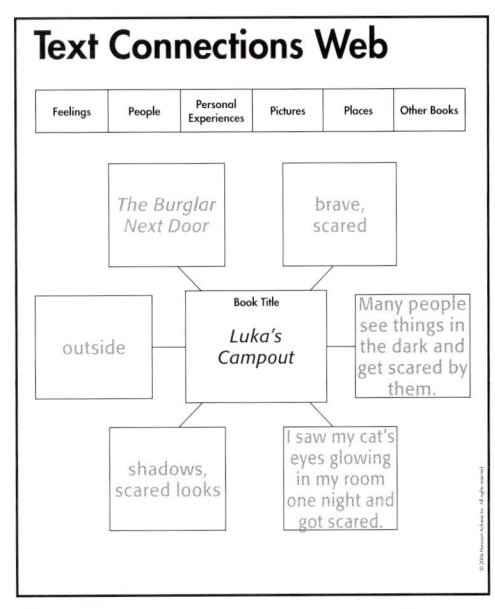

Text Connections Web

Feelings | People | Personal Experiences | Pictures | Places | Other Books

- The Burglar Next Door
- brave, scared
- outside
- **Book Title:** Luka's Campout
- Many people see things in the dark and get scared by them.
- shadows, scared looks
- I saw my cat's eyes glowing in my room one night and got scared.

Directions: With children, fill in the Text Connections Web for *Luka's Campout*.

Discussion Questions

- What kept Luka from getting any sleep? (Literal)
- How was Luka's campout different from what he expected? (Critical Thinking)
- Will Luka be less afraid on his next campout? Why? (Inferential)

T7

Activity Sheets

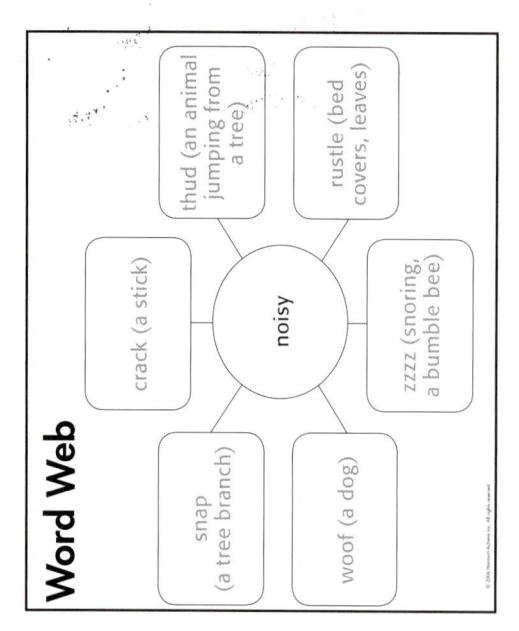

Word Web

- thud (an animal jumping from a tree)
- rustle (bed covers, leaves)
- zzzz (snoring, a bumble bee)
- woof (a dog)
- snap (a tree branch)
- crack (a stick)

Center: **noisy**

Directions: Have children fill in the Word Web using the word *noisy*. Include descriptions of things that can make each noise.

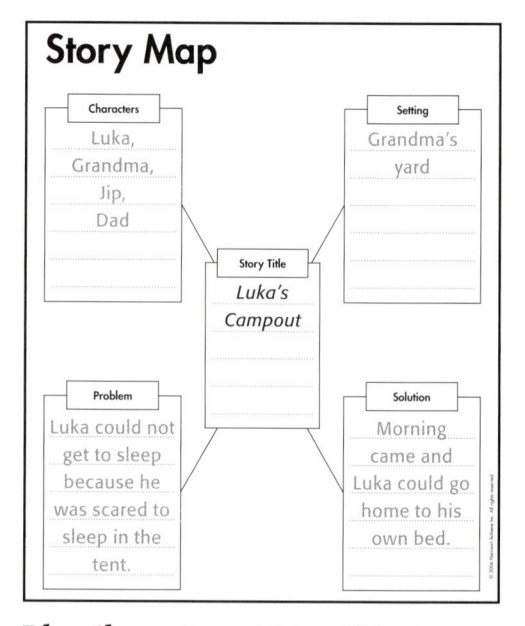

Story Map

Characters: Luka, Grandma, Jip, Dad

Setting: Grandma's yard

Story Title: Luka's Campout

Problem: Luka could not get to sleep because he was scared to sleep in the tent.

Solution: Morning came and Luka could go home to his own bed.

Directions: Have children fill in the Story Map for *Luka's Campout*. Optional: Have children use the Story Map to find a phrase in the text and copy it.